CW00919522

by Iain Gray

WRITING *to* REMEMBER

Lang**Syne**

PUBLISHING

WRITING *to* REMEMBER

79 Main Street, Newtongrange,
Midlothian EH22 4NA
Tel: 0131 344 0414   Fax: 0845 075 6085
E-mail: info@lang-syne.co.uk
www.langsyneshop.co.uk

Design by Dorothy Meikle
Printed by Ricoh Print Scotland
© Lang Syne Publishers Ltd 2015

ISBN 978-1-85217-545-0

Thompson

MOTTO:
Know thyself.

CREST:
A lion holding a lure.

NAME variations include:
Tamson
Thomson
Tomson
Thomsoun

Chapter one:

The origins of popular surnames

by George Forbes and Iain Gray

If you don't know where you came from, you won't know where you're going is a frequently quoted observation and one that has a particular resonance today when there has been a marked upsurge in interest in genealogy, with increasing numbers of people curious to trace their family roots.

Main sources for genealogical research include census returns and official records of births, marriages and deaths – and the key to unlocking the detail they contain is obviously a family surname, one that has been 'inherited' and passed from generation to generation.

No matter our station in life, we all have a surname – but it was not until about the middle of the fourteenth century that the practice of being identified by a particular surname became commonly established throughout the British Isles.

Previous to this, it was normal for a person to be identified through the use of only a forename.

But as population gradually increased and there were many more people with the same forename, surnames were adopted to distinguish one person, or community, from another.

Many common English surnames are patronymic in origin, meaning they stem from the forename of one's father – with 'Johnson,' for example, indicating 'son of John.'

It was the Normans, in the wake of their eleventh century conquest of Anglo-Saxon England, a pivotal moment in the nation's history, who first brought surnames into usage – although it was a gradual process.

For the Normans, these were names initially based on the title of their estates, local villages and chateaux in France to distinguish and identify these landholdings.

Such grand descriptions also helped enhance the prestige of these warlords and generally glorify their lofty positions high above the humble serfs slaving away below in the pecking order who had only single names, often with Biblical connotations as in Pierre and Jacques.

The only descriptive distinctions among the peasantry concerned their occupations, like 'Pierre the swineherd' or 'Jacques the ferryman.'

Roots of surnames that came into usage in England not only included Norman-French, but also Old French, Old Norse, Old English, Middle English, German, Latin, Greek, Hebrew and the Gaelic languages of the Celts.

The Normans themselves were originally Vikings, or 'Northmen', who raided, colonised and eventually settled down around the French coastline.

The had sailed up the Seine in their longboats in 900AD under their ferocious leader Rollo and ruled the roost in north eastern France before sailing over to conquer England in 1066 under Duke William of Normandy – better known to posterity as William the Conqueror, or King William I of England.

Granted lands in the newly-conquered England, some of their descendants later acquired territories in Wales, Scotland and Ireland – taking not only their own surnames, but also the practice of adopting a surname, with them.

But it was in England where Norman rule and custom first impacted, particularly in relation to the adoption of surnames.

This is reflected in the famous *Domesday Book*, a massive survey of much of England and Wales, ordered by William I, to determine who owned what, what it was worth and therefore how much they were liable to pay in taxes to the voracious Royal Exchequer.

Completed in 1086 and now held in the National Archives in Kew, London, 'Domesday' was an Old English word meaning 'Day of Judgement.'

This was because, in the words of one contemporary chronicler, "its decisions, like those of the Last Judgement, are unalterable."

It had been a requirement of all those English landholders – from the richest to the poorest – that they identify themselves for the purposes of the survey and for future reference by means of a surname.

This is why the *Domesday Book*, although written in Latin as was the practice for several centuries with both civic and ecclesiastical records, is an invaluable source for the early appearance of a wide range of English surnames.

Several of these names were coined in connection with occupations.

These include Baker and Smith, while Cooks, Chamberlains, Constables and Porters were to be found carrying out duties in large medieval households.

The church's influence can be found in names such as Bishop, Friar and Monk while the popular name of Bennett derives from the late fifth to mid-sixth century Saint Benedict, founder of the Benedictine order of monks.

The early medical profession is represented by Barber, while businessmen produced names that include Merchant and Sellers.

Down at the village watermill, the names that cropped up included Millar/Miller, Walker and Fuller, while other self-explanatory trades included Cooper, Tailor, Mason and Wright.

Even the scenery was utilised as in Moor, Hill, Wood and Forrest – while the hunt and the chase supplied names that include Hunter, Falconer, Fowler and Fox.

Colours are also a source of popular surnames, as in Black, Brown, Gray/Grey, Green and White, and would have denoted the colour of the clothing the person habitually wore or, apart from the obvious exception of 'Green', one's hair colouring or even complexion.

The surname Red developed into Reid, while

Blue was rare and no-one wanted to be associated with yellow.

Rather self-important individuals took surnames that include Goodman and Wiseman, while physical attributes crept into surnames such as Small and Little.

Many families proudly boast the heraldic device known as a Coat of Arms, as featured on our front cover.

The central motif of the Coat of Arms would originally have been what was borne on the shield of a warrior to distinguish himself from others on the battlefield.

Not featured on the Coat of Arms, but high-lighted on page three, is the family motto and related crest – with the latter frequently different from the central motif.

Adding further variety to the rich cultural heritage that is represented by surnames is the appearance in recent times in lists of the 100 most common names found in England of ones that include Khan, Patel and Singh – names that have proud roots in the vast sub-continent of India.

Echoes of a far distant past can still be found in our surnames and they can be borne with pride in commemoration of our forebears.

Chapter two:

Ancient roots

A surname that stems from the popular forename 'Thomas' or the earlier 'Thom', 'Thompson' indicates 'son of Thomas' or 'son of Thom.'

Of Middle Eastern roots, the given name of Thomas originally indicated 'twin.'

Ranked at 15th in some lists of the 100 most common surnames found in England today, bearers of its spelling variant of 'Thomson', ranked at 81st, have their own proud history and traditions.

With Thompson being a name first popularised throughout England by the Anglo-Saxons, this means that flowing through the veins of many of its bearers today is the blood of those Germanic tribes who invaded and settled in the south and east of the island of Britain from about the early fifth century.

Known as the Anglo-Saxons, they were composed of the Jutes, from the area of the Jutland Peninsula in modern Denmark, the Saxons from Lower Saxony, in modern Germany and the Angles from the Angeln area of Germany.

It was the Angles who gave the name 'Engla land', or 'Aengla land' – better known as 'England.'

They held sway in what became known as England from approximately 550 to 1066, with the main kingdoms those of Sussex, Wessex, Northumbria, Mercia, Kent, East Anglia and Essex.

Whoever controlled the most powerful of these kingdoms was tacitly recognised as overall 'king' – one of the most noted being Alfred the Great, King of Wessex from 871 to 899.

It was during his reign that the famous *Anglo-Saxon Chronicle* was compiled – an invaluable source of Anglo-Saxon history – while Alfred was designated in early documents as *Rex Anglorum Saxonum*, King of the English Saxons. Other important Anglo-Saxon works include the epic *Beowulf* and the seventh century *Caedmon's Hymn*.

The Anglo-Saxons meanwhile, had usurped the power of the indigenous Britons – who referred to them as 'Saeson' or 'Saxones.'

It is from this that the Scottish Gaelic term for 'English people' of 'Sasannach' derives, the Irish Gaelic 'Sasanach' and the Welsh 'Saeson.'

We learn from the *Anglo-Saxon Chronicle* how the religion of the early Anglo-Saxons, including those who would later adopt the Thompson name, was one that pre-dated the establishment of Christianity in the British Isles. Known as a form of Germanic paganism, with roots in Old Norse religion, it shared much in common with the Druidic 'nature-worshipping' religion of the indigenous Britons.

It was in the closing years of the sixth century that Christianity began to take a hold in Britain, while by approximately 690 it had become the 'established' religion of Anglo-Saxon England.

The death knell of Anglo-Saxon supremacy was sounded in the wake of the Norman Conquest of 1066 – a key event in English history.

By this date, England had become a nation with several powerful competitors to the throne and in what were extremely complex family, political and military machinations, the monarch was Harold II, who had succeeded to the throne following the death of Edward the Confessor.

But his right to the throne was contested by two powerful competitors – his brother-in-law King Harold Hardrada of Norway, in alliance with Tostig, Harold II's brother, and Duke William II of Normandy.

In what has become known as The Year of Three Battles, Hardrada invaded England and gained victory over the English king on September 20 at the battle of Fulford, in Yorkshire.

Five days later, however, Harold II decisively defeated his brother-in-law and brother at the battle of Stamford Bridge. But he had little time to celebrate his victory, having to immediately march south from Yorkshire to encounter a mighty invasion force, led by Duke William of Normandy, that had landed at Hastings, in East Sussex.

Harold's battle-hardened but exhausted force confronted the Normans on October 14 in a battle subsequently depicted on the Bayeux tapestry – a 23ft. long strip of embroidered linen thought to have been commissioned eleven years after the event by the Norman Odo of Bayeux.

It was at the top of Senlac Hill that Harold drew up a strong defensive position, building a shield wall to repel Duke William's cavalry and infantry.

The Normans suffered heavy losses, but through a combination of the deadly skill of their archers and the ferocious determination of their cavalry they eventually won the day.

Anglo-Saxon morale had collapsed on the battlefield as word spread through the ranks that Harold had been killed – the Bayeux Tapestry depicting this as having happened when the English king was struck by an arrow to the head.

Amidst the carnage of the battlefield, it was difficult to identify him – the last of the Anglo-Saxon kings. Some sources assert William ordered his body to be thrown into the sea, while others state it was secretly buried at Waltham Abbey.

What is known with certainty, however, is that William in celebration of his great victory founded Battle Abbey, near the site of the battle, ordering that the altar be sited on the spot where Harold was believed to have fallen.

William was declared King of England on December 25 and the subjugation of his Anglo-Saxon subjects such as the Thompsons followed.

Within an astonishingly short space of time, Norman manners, customs and law were imposed on England – laying the basis for what subsequently became established 'English' custom and practice.

But Anglo-Saxon culture was not totally eradicated, with some aspects absorbed into that of the Normans, while faint echoes of its proud and colourful past is still seen today in the form of popular surnames such as Thompson.

The name is first found in what for centuries

was the north-western English territory of Cumberland – which since local government reorganisation in 1974 now forms, along with Westmoreland and parts of northern Lancashire, the administrative region of Cumbria.

It was in Cumberland, original heartland of bearers of the Thompson name, that for centuries they lived an often precarious and violent existence.

The name of Cumberland first appears in 945 A.D. with the *Anglo-Saxon Chronicle* recording that this was when the area was ceded to Scotland's Malcolm I by England's King Edmund.

Carlisle, that in its own right formed an important part of Cumberland, was invaded by England's William Rufus in 1092 and, constantly battled over in a series of bloody conflicts, was again regained by Scotland under David I; its blood-stained soil was then recaptured for England in 1157 under Henry II.

Living in close and hostile proximity to Scotland, bearers of the Thompson name were for centuries engaged in vicious Border warfare.

Known on both sides of the border as 'reivers', the Thompsons and others took this name from their lawless custom of 'reiving', or raiding, not only their neighbours' livestock, but also that of their neighbours across the border.

The word 'bereaved', for example, indicating to have suffered loss, derives from the original 'reived', meaning to have suffered loss of property.

A constant thorn in the flesh of both the English and Scottish authorities was the cross-border raiding and pillaging carried out by well-mounted and heavily armed men, the contingent from the Scottish side of the border known and feared as 'moss troopers.'

In an attempt to bring order to what was known as the wild 'debateable land' on both sides of the border, in 1237 Alexander II of Scotland signed the Treaty of York, which for the first time established the Scottish border with England as a line running from the Solway to the Tweed.

On either side of the border there were three 'marches' or areas of administration, the West, East, and Middle Marches, and a warden governed these.

Complaints from either side of the border were dealt with on Truce Days, when the wardens of the different marches would act as arbitrators – while there was also a law known as the Hot Trod, that granted anyone who had their livestock stolen the right to pursue the thieves and recover their property.

Chapter three:

Science and adventure

In rather more peaceful times, bearers of the Thompson name feature prominently in the historical record – particularly as pioneering scientists and adventurers.

A Fellow of the prestigious scientific 'think-tank' known as the Royal Society and of the Royal Society of Edinburgh, Thomas Thompson was the Scottish chemist and mineralogist who in 1817 gave the name to the chemical element 'silicon.'

Born in 1773 in Crieff, Perthshire, and after having studied classics, mathematics and natural philosophy at St Andrews University and then graduating with a degree in medicine from Edinburgh University, he went on to publish a number of important works.

These include his 1802 *Survey of Chemistry* and the 1810 *The Elements of Chemistry*.

Latterly Professor of Chemistry at Glasgow University and an early researcher into atomic theory, he died in 1852.

Born in Edinburgh in 1860, Sir D'Arcy Wentworth Thompson was the biologist who because of his landmark 1917 *On Growth and Form*, was awarded twelve years after his death in 1948 a Nobel Laureate in Medicine for "the finest work of literature in all the annals of science that have been recorded by the English tongue."

The book is famed for having defined 'morphogenesis – the complex process by which distinctive patterns are formed in both plants and animals.

A graduate of both Edinburgh University and Cambridge University and a Fellow of the Royal Society, he was also the recipient of many other scientific honours that include the Darwin Medal and the Daniel Giruad Elliot Medal from America's National Academy of Sciences.

Not only a pioneering physicist but also a noted inventor, Sir Benjamin Thompson, also known as Count Rumford, was born in 1753 in Woburn, Massachusetts, to British immigrants to America.

Best known for theories that revolutionised the understanding of thermodynamics, he was the author of the important 1798 *An Experimental Enquiry Concerning the Source of Heat which is Excited by Friction*, while his second wife was Marie-Anne Lavoisier, widow of the famous French chemist Antoine Lavoisier.

Receiving a knighthood in the Peerage of the United Kingdom in 1784 after having served as a Lieutenant-Colonel in the Loyalist forces during the American Revolutionary War of 1775 to 1783, he later moved to Bavaria to continue his scientific studies.

It was here that he was honoured as a Count of the Holy Roman Empire, taking the title of Reichsgraf von Rumford – Baron Rumford – with 'Rumford' the name of the town in America's New Hampshire where he had married his first wife, Sarah Rolfe.

A prolific inventor, before his death in 1814 he devised not only a forerunner of today's coffee percolator, but also improvements to household chimneys and industrial furnaces.

The Moon crater *Rumford* is named in his honour, while in his lifetime he endowed the Rumford Medals of the American Academy of Arts and Sciences and of the Royal Society, in addition to endowing a professorship at Harvard University.

He was the father, through his first marriage, of Sarah Thompson, Countess Rumford, born in 1774 in New Hampshire.

It was after her father's death that, inheriting

the title of Countess Rumford, she became the first American to be known as a countess; a philanthropist who spent her time in homes she owned not only in her native New Hampshire but also in Paris and London, she died in 1852.

In the world of contemporary science, Kenneth Lane Thompson, born in New Orleans in 1943, is the leading American computer scientist better known as Ken Thompson.

It was while working for Bell Labs that in 1969 he designed and implemented the famous *UNIX* operating system, while he also invented the *B programming* computer language; the recipient of a number of awards that include the Turing Award and America's National Medal of Technology, he has worked since 2006 with the Internet research engine company *Google*.

Recognised as having been "the greatest land geographer who ever lived", David Thompson was the British-Canadian fur trader, surveyor and map-maker born in Westminster, London, in 1770.

His father died when he was aged two and, because of his family's subsequent financial hardship, he and his brother were placed in a school for the disadvantaged.

This was to prove of great benefit to him, for it was here that he honed the mathematical skills that formed the basis for his future career as a surveyor and map-maker.

Apprenticed to the Hudson's Bay Company in North America, he spent some time in Manitoba where he studied surveying under the guidance of the company's leading surveyor Philip Turnor.

Having completed his apprenticeship when he was aged 20, he was then employed by them as a fur trader.

But, also utilising his impressive surveying and map-making skills, he completed a survey in 1792 that mapped a route to Lake Athabasca, on the border of what is now Alberta and Saskatchewan.

Leaving the Hudson's Bay Company in 1797 and joining its rival the North West Company, he went on to map much of the interior of what later would become known as Canada.

Known to native peoples he met on his surveying and map-making expeditions as "Koo-Koo-Sint" – "Stargazer" – it is estimated that before his death in 1857 he had mapped a North American land mass amounting to nearly four million square kilometres.

Despite his achievements, he died in relative obscurity, and it was not until 1916 that his field notebooks were collated and published by J.B. Tyrell as *David Thompson's Narrative*.

Honoured by the Canadian Government in 1957 with his image on a postage stamp, the David Thompson Highway in Alberta is also named in his honour.

Yet another intrepid traveller, this time on the high seas, was the rather oddly named John Sen Inches Thompson, the Scottish ship owner, sea captain, whaler and author born in 1845 in Alloa, Clackmannan.

It was after his marriage to Margaret Inches, of Blairgowrie, Perthshire, that he added her surname to his own name.

He is best known for a voyage he took in 1877, aboard the *Bencleugh*, when he and his crew were shipwrecked after a violent gale off Macquarie Island, Tasmania.

Leading a perilous existence on the island and on the brink of starvation, it was four long months later that they were eventually rescued by the *Bencleugh's* sister ship, *Friendship*.

His book, *Voyages and Wanderings in Far*

Off Lands, was published just over 20 years before his death in 1933.

Two infamous bearers of the Thompson name were the American Old West gambler, gunman and lawman Ben Thompson and his younger brother Billy, also known as "Texas Billy."

Born in 1843 in Knottingley, West Yorkshire Ben and his brother, born in 1845, immigrated with their parents to America in 1852, eventually settling in Austin, Texas.

Working for a time as a printer's assistant on an Austin newspaper, Ben Thompson eventually turned to gambling as a career, travelling throughout the length and breadth of the Unites States from one gambling den and saloon to another.

Enlisting during the American Civil War of 1861 to 1865 in the 2nd Regiment, Texas Mounted Rifles, of the Confederate States Army, along with his brother, it was shortly after the conflict began that the volatile Ben shot two men in a row over rations.

In 1868, after shooting his brother-in-law over a family feud, he spent some time in prison before being pardoned.

By 1871, he had opened the Bull's Head saloon in Abilene, Kansas and it was here that he made the acquaintance of other legendary Old West characters who included John Wesley Hardin, Marshall "Wild Bill" Hickok, "Buffalo Bill" Cody and Bat Masterton.

Later re-locating to Austin, Texas, and despite his reputation as a gunman – or perhaps because of it – he was appointed town marshal.

He was killed, in a hail of bullets, after becoming embroiled in a feud in a theatre in San Antonio in 1884; his equally volatile brother Billy died in 1897.

In the world of politics, Sir John Thompson, born in 1845 in Halifax, Nova Scotia, was the lawyer, judge, university professor and politician who served as 4th Prime Minister of Canada from 1892 until his death in office two years later.

Born in 1961, David Thompson served as 6th Prime Minister of Barbados from 2008 until his death in 2010.

A leading British historian and peace campaigner, Edward Palmer Thompson, better known as E.P. Thompson, was born in 1924 and is best known for his renowned 1963 book *The Making of the English Working Class*.

A prominent member of the Communist

Party of Great Britain until he left it in 1956 following the Soviet invasion of Hungary, he nevertheless remained a noted Marxist historian.

Also a member and campaigner for the Campaign for Nuclear Disarmament (CND), and the author of a number of biographies and a collection of poetry, he died in 1993.

Through his marriage to fellow historian and peace activist Dorothy Towers, he was the father of the award-winning British writer of children's novels Kate Thompson.

Born in 1956 in Halifax, Yorkshire, her 2005 *The New Policemen* won both the Whitbread Children's Book Award and the Guardian Children's Fiction Prize.

Chapter four:

On the world stage

Born in 1959 in Paddington, London, Emma Thompson is the multi-award-winning British actress, screenwriter and author who first came to prominence in 1987 for her roles in the BBC television series *Tutti Frutti* and *Fortunes of War*.

The recipient of a BAFTA Awards for Best Actress for work in both of these series, her first major screen credit was the 1989 romantic comedy *The Tall Guy*.

Also the recipient in 1992 of an Academy Award and a BAFTA for Best Actress for her role in *Howard's End*, her many other awards include an Academy Award for Best Adapted Screenplay for the 1995 *Sense and Sensibility* – which she both scripted and starred in.

The daughter of the actor and director Eric Thompson, who wrote the British television children's series *The Magic Roundabout*, and the Scottish actress Phyllida Law, her other screen credits include the 2003 *Love Actually* and the 2005 *Nanny McPhee*.

Married from 1989 to 1995 to the actor

Kenneth Branagh, she is also the older sister of the actress Sophie Thompson.

On American shores, **Ron Thompson** is the actor of stage, television and film who won the Los Angeles Drama Critics Circle Award in 1973 for his role in the play *Does a Tiger Wear a Necktie?*

Born in 1941 in Louisville, Kentucky, his television credits include *Ironside*, *The Streets of San Francisco* and *Baretta*, while big screen credits include the 1973 *The No Mercy Men*, the 1981 *American Pop* and, from 1998, *Fallen Arches*.

With television credits that include *The X-Files*, *Star Trek: Voyager* and *Dark Frontier*, **Susanna Thompson** is the American actress born in 1958 in San Diego, California.

Her film credits include the 1994 *Little Giants*, the 1996 *Ghosts of Mississippi* and, from 2002, *Dragonfly*.

The recipient of a star on the Hollywood Walk of Fame, **Bill Thompson** was the famed American radio and voice actor who, in 1937, created the radio character of the mild-mannered Wallace Wimple.

Born in 1913 in Terre Haute, Indiana, before his death in 1971 he was known as the 'voice' for a number of television and film characters who included the the White Rabbit and Dodo in Disney's *Alice in Wonderland* and as King Hubert in *Sleeping Beauty*.

Born in 1950, **David Thompson** is the British television and film producer who, after joining the BBC in 1978 and working as a film programmer and documentary maker, was later instrumental in the set-up of BBC Films.

Other projects in which he has been involved include the 2006 film *The History Boys* and the 2008 remake of *Brideshead Revisited*.

Bearers of the Thompson name have also excelled in the highly competitive world of sport – no less so than the great British former athlete **Daley Thompson**.

Born Francis Morgan Ayodélé Thompson in Notting Hill, London, in 1958, to a Scottish mother and a Nigerian father, a taxi driver, who was shot dead on the streets of the Streatham area of London when Daley was aged about 12.

Putting his troubled past behind him, he went on to become one of the greatest decathletes the world has ever seen.

His many awards include winning the gold

medal at the 1980 and 1984 Olympic Games, breaking the world record in the event four times and winning the gold medal in the 1978, 1982 and 1986 Commonwealth Games.

Also the winner of the gold medal at the 1982 and 1986 European Championships, he was forced to retire from athletics in 1992 due to injury.

The recipient of the 1982 BBC Sports Personality of the Year Award and an MBE, OBE and CBE, he played professional football for a time following his retirement from athletics for teams that included Mansfield Town. He also served as an ambassador for the 2012 Olympic Games in London.

From athletics to rugby, **Duncan Thompson** was the Australian rugby league player and coach regarded as having been 'the father of modern coaching.'

Born in 1895 in Warwick, Queensland, the talented half-back's career was interrupted with military service on the Western Front during the First World War. Shot through the chest in April of 1918, but surviving the ordeal despite having a bullet fragment lodged in his body, he was told he would never be able to play sport again.

But despite this he went on to play in the

1921-1922 Kangaroo Tour of Great Britain and, turning his talents for a time to tennis, playing in the men's doubles event at the 1931 New South Wales Open.

Also an administrator for the Queensland Rugby League and a coach for the Toowoomba Clydesdales, leading them to six victories in the 1950s, and an inductee of the Australian Rugby League Hall of Fame, he died in 1980.

Born in Glasgow in 1940, **Eddie Thompson** was the Scottish businessman who took over control of Scottish football club Dundee United in 2002, serving as its chairman until his death in a road accident in 2008.

From sport to the world of music, two bearers of the Thompson name are noted contemporary rock drummers.

Born in Glasgow in 1976, **Paul Thompson** is the drummer for the internationally best-selling band Franz Ferdinand, while his namesake, **Paul Thompson**, born in 1951 in Newcastle upon Tyne, was the drummer from 1971 to 1980 and then from 2001 of the band Roxy Music.

On the saxophone, **Lee Jay Thompson**, born in London in 1957, is the musician best known as a member of the band Madness, first formed in 1976, and some of whose hits, written or co-written by Thompson, include *Embarrassment* and *Razor Blade Alley*.

From music to the written word, Hunter Stockton Thompson was the American journalist and author better known as **Hunter S. Thompson**. Born in 1937 in Louisville, Kentucky, he became famous for pioneering what is known as New Journalism – or, in his own words, "Gonzo" journalism, and a style in which the reporter becomes intimately involved on a personal level with the particular story.

After having lived for a time with a group of American motorcyclists known as Hell's Angels, he published his *Hell's Angels: The Strange and Terrible Saga of the Outlaw Motorcycle Gangs in 1967*. He is best known, however, for his 1972 *Fear and Loathing in Las Vegas: A Savage Journey to the Heart of the American Dream*, later adapted for the 1998 film *Fear and Loathing in Las Vegas*, starring Johnny Depp.

He took his own life in August of 2005 and, in keeping with what had been his unconventional lifestyle, his ashes were fired from a cannon to the tunes of Norman Greenbaum's *Spirit in the Sky* and Bob Dylan's *Mr Tambourine Man*.